orange fire

poems by
Judith R. Robinson

MAIN STREET RAG PUBLISHING COMPANY
CHARLOTTE, NORTH CAROLINA

Library of Congress Control Number: 2012953874

ISBN: 978-1-59948-389-4

Produced in the United States of America

Main Street Rag
PO Box 690100
Charlotte, NC 28227
www.MAINSTREETRAG.COM

ACKNOWLEDGMENTS:

Along These Rivers: Poetry and Photography from Pittsburgh:
"In Stilettos"
Blue Unicorn: "Gone, Goodbye, Encore," "Airborne,"
"Dear Jim," "Translucence"
ByLine: "To Write"
California Quarterly: "Black Scar" (first appeared as "Vietnam
Memorial")
Eye Contact: "Lesson," "Numbness"
5 AM: "I Apologize," "At Lanigan's"
Jane's Stories: "A Catholic Funeral"
The Main Street Rag: "Nineteen-Fifty-Six," "Ravages"
Midstream: "Yad Vashem"
Carnegie Library Natural Language: "Two Thousand Twelve"
(first appeared as "Two Thousand Nine")
Only the Sea Keeps: Poetry of the Tsunami: "The Human Wave"
The Pittsburgh Post-Gazette: "Dream Lunch," "It Is Everywhere
Blues," "To Civility," "Unseasonable," "January," 'April,"
"Tulips"
The Pittsburgh Quarterly: "Child's Play," "Vineyard,"
"Magicians," "Pink Lady," "Rage," "Bed and Breakfast"
Poetica: "I Apologize," "A Survivor's Child Paints,"
"1945 Song," "This Story" "Yad Vashem"
The Poetry Ark: "Old Loves"
The Raystown Review: "Sister Woman," "Heather"
Rockhurst Review: "Heaven," "Numbness"
Rune: "O, The Nice Things," "Bitter Rain," "Numbness"

Some of the poems that appear in *Orange Fire* also appeared in
the chapbook, *Dinner Date,* published by Finishing Line Press in
2009.

A prose poem version of "A Catholic Funeral" won first prize in
the Jane's Story Drabble Competition in 2007.

"Songs," "Yad Vashem," "1945 Song," and "Bitter Rain" have been
reprinted in the anthologies, *Voices Israel, 2010,* edited by Michael
Dickel, and *Voices Israel, 2011,* edited by Jon Michael Simon.

"1945 Song" was reprinted in the *Mizmor L'David Anthology*, 2010, edited by Michal Mahgerefteh.

"At Lanigan's," "A Survivor's Child Paints," "Numbness," and "Ravages" were reprinted in *5 Poetry Journal*, 2011, edited by Libby Hart.

"I Apologize" won the Reuben Rose International Poetry Competition, 2011, second place.

for my beloved son
Sanford N. Robinson, Jr.

CONTENTS

AT LANIGAN'S

The body lies
neatly clothed,
the face
powdered as well
as possible, being
so dead now.
Clearly, the soul has fled,
with its grace
and kindness. Now
mourning is somewhere
else too. Not here
with this strange
shell, this imposter.

THE 50S

In the middle
of the 20th
century
before God
decided
to leave

adults
wore hats
smoked cigarettes
placed teeth
white as
shirt buttons
in cups
at night
watched Ike
play golf
on newsreels
& didn't bother
to lock
doors;

God could not
have faulted them
this foolishness

could He?

NINETEEN FIFTY-SIX

hard dirt & stones

around my tree—a telley pole

with lots of jaggy nails

our yard hangs over

US STEEL

it always rains

puddles up the holes

where long gray

worms stretch

even longer

& tiny dragons float

dead at night

i love it when

the sky burns up

no smoke

just orange fire

JULY 1958

I saw my mother swaying
on the front lawn
nothing to hold onto
before she crumbled into
a heap of person in a housedress
on the grass & the neighbor
Old Wilson came running

from his porch to move her
out of the way
as the cops took aim
& shot at the scampering rats
which they zinged to death

all four big ones popped up
before they fell down—
none swayed—they just went up
into the blue air
outlines of the rats they were
in the air for a split second.

I wondered if my mother
would be the same as before.
I knew that those rats
would be hard to forget.

CHILD'S PLAY

Where is Billy Applebee, our tormentor?
And what stopped our game, Tar-Baby Stop?
A little girl, fingers tingling,
Running, desperate for the ball, and then
A getting-so-much-bigger girl
(how you've grown!)
aching with secrets.

Day slipping into forbidden night.
To be big enough to stay out there!
Badly wanting and not wanting
Everything waiting in the dark
To kiss and capture and devour.

Wait, stop, please wait.
I turned my foolish head to see you
And the summer years blinked by.
There's some injustice here
It isn't fair
Look, let's just take it over.

O, THE NICE THINGS

Her cures included
Nice things
A nice bath
A nice cup of lemon tea
A nice story
As if coziness
Was the antidote
To the line-up
Of heart stings
That revealed
Who you
Really were:
Fat, unfriended
Unkissed
Middle school
Zero and O yes
Desperado
Aching to
Need to wear
A bra.

HAWAIIAN NIGHT

The singles won't mingle
quite yet. The used-to-be-boys

cluster in corners
the tall & the short

clutching piña coladas
laugh out loud over nothing

as the ladies, lit up by torches,
chatter & flutter, hens among palms.

This here's the Days Inn party room,
exhorts the bald Dee-jay, *so get up & dance!*

Do they wish to be here?
All of them must; so much has ended

yet something remains; hearts scabbed
over are hearts just the same.

WHEN WANTING

what pleads
inside to stop

take a walk
on hot sand

you know you are
somewhere

your feet
burn so badly

that uncertainty
has no purchase.

When you are cut
or cut yourself

the focus shifts
from inside

& pain moves
out with it.

A hatchling
blossoms before you.

The dog watching
these ferocious

operations understands.
He is smart enough &

wears the mark of
a perfect black heart.

STAY

1

Where have you gone, dearest M?

I think you are
hiding deep in the woods,

& I intend to find you.

You will not see me coming—

your eyes sealed
under thick buckeye branches,

asleep or awake you never admit
anything, neither fear nor love,

but my blood pulses so

seeing you, I swear I know
what is needed.

2

I whisper: awaken to me;
inhale the perfume
of these last flowers,
orange petals drooped and curling,

soft dark vines around us, one more

dawn
coming on.

3

Still, summer's end surrounds
you with the heaviness

of unsaid thought. I ask you
to remember different days,

the long shadowed hours
of June, impressions
of earliness, fists of buds,

yellow birds bathing
in the garden.

4

Some other sun rises
much too late, drenches
the leaves
in startling heat-waves

then seeks us out, I imagine.

But there is no promise
in the bleaching

no bargains, nothing
to wet our cracked lips.

Cuckoo birds screech
& flee into
old buckeye trees.

Now, in the closeness,
when nothing left
breathes or stirs,
in vain I plead stay,
stay summer, stay you,
stay.

UNBINDING

for Rosaly Roffman

A cold night, slick streets,
milky snow; we complain a little
then listen to the Greek
poems set to music:
Saranda! A voice, in agony;
a wail we know, a sob that's
whispered; strings that grieve,
bells that beat against the heart.

Ritsos, dazed, imprisoned on an island;
Ritsos, looking out at the Aegean,
opening his mouth to find
wretchedness green as leaves pour forth.

To be free for just one hour!
To thrust the head into blessed fog,
to feel life move as a river.
To lie down on grass and mingle
hot sweat with dew,
tears with stones, dear God!

We are stunned, gutted as fish.

Slowly we weave our way out;
blink back into the deep night.
The wet sky has cleared,
the Oakland street is wide open.

We breathe in the cold.
Rosaly takes my arm.

The dying Greek stays with us.

DREAM LUNCH

for Grant

I'd like to write
a poem when I'm hungry
stomach firing
up the imagination

with aromas of steaming pans
of glowing yellow onions
frying, buttery, turning crisp;

or purple onions sliced over
tender summer greens, arugula or bibb,
chunks of blue-veined cheese
with oil that soaked the Tuscan sun

and Morton's kosher salt.
And yes, I'd like some
hearty, heavy bread
brown and crusty, embedded

with sesame seeds & lots
of crunchy nuts, walnut, pine,
and such. Let me add some

ripe tomato from the garden
tended since spring
by the dearest little soul

I know, who would like
some peanut butter & jelly.

THE NEW TECH

Soon in this sparse world
There won't be anyone
Born like Rootie
Who ran around
On errands for Sol
Repeating *Gotta dime? Gotta dime?*
Or Epps who always
Wore Sunday clothes,
A fancy snap brim hat;
Or the lady-man
With the mustache,
Hairy arms in a see-through dress;
All of them who
Spoke in secrets smiling
To themselves
And scared you good when
You were a just a kid
Out on the avenue.

IT IS EVERYWHERE BLUES

American original O most beautiful
Restless leaping
That spews
Another, and another
And still more ...

So goodbye bumpy playground—

Hello Pretenders hello

Pretend
You're happy when you're blue
It isn't very hard to do...

Chevy Impala
Put that old soft top down
Bring back Elvis
Put him on the tube
Bury him again.

Listen in, sports fans: It isn't over 'til it's over:

My new hometown—McCity, Colorado
My new stomping grounds—McMall, Pennsylvania
My old Ma and Pa—McGated, Florida

So what if nothing's really?

It's here & very clean
Brighter than it used to be
And you rarely need to think
Keeps you moving
Keeps you dazzled.

Let the next years come, babe
Let the past years go—

Just as if you had a choice.

TWO-THOUSAND-TWELVE

I love to see
the flowers tier out front—

crocus first, then
happy yellow daffs,

tulips, elegant ladies
too tall and cool to remain

past April. At last azaleas
burst gaudy free

& then suddenly

Spring is gone

and so too my neighbor's tree
the bold Sweet Gum—

so audacious!
bearing leaves in five glowing colors

spreading roots, disrupting the flow
of city sewers,

so outrageous

it had to be killed, cut down,
its criminal stump

dragged off in chains.

What scant violation is this?

Weapons cut down
innocents and masses somewhere

starve. The television keeps blinking.

This is two-thousand and twelve.

I am far too old to weep for trees.

TO CIVILITY: APRIL

Clouds, shaded soft
as dove's wings,
yield most days
to showers, sometimes fresh,
but often harsh,
piercing

as the first shocked
days of mourning,

as when violent spring
rains moisture
upon the cold earth,
heaps wetness
on us all, lies heavy
on the chilled trees,

as well as the children;

drenches them
green and thick-skinned
forcing growth along the broken streets,
streets of bricks and holes and wires
without the steady
sun of other places.

Sturdy sprouts never hide
in the spare gray light,
the long sweep of wind:
they learn early
to stretch, to climb, to bob up and bloom;
if some are shaken, tumbled,
uncontained, they are searched out,
they are found.

LOSING THE SUGAR

Yearning comes: a wide, blue tide,
like the Aegean, advancing, invading
a pure white beach,
salt aching to consume sugar.

There is a game going on—
like soft sand and sea tide—
pull/resist, resist/pull,
cycle after cycle of play
& time seems to have a part—

as does wind, bird, & sun.
How much will be taken,
how much surrendered,
before the day itself is lost?

The dipping sun casts
darkness against the pale sand:
one twined shape rising, falling,
the he and she breathing
deep the salt, losing the sugar.

Nothing disturbs the rhythm.
He joins the breeze unleashing
her hair. They consume
and are consumed, folding,
unfolding, folding.

APRIL

They weep,
the sweet unsprung buds.
They cringe
and hide, perilously
bent beneath
skies restless and dark
as widow's weeds
as rivers rise
in western Pennsylvania.
Does this gloom
portend a raging death
or will it yield to
something tender?
Shall we weep with them
or wait? When I was young
and clear and wise
I knew the answer:
Hold fast, I'd say, tomorrow
comes in green and gold
and you and I will lust
and live forever.

IN STILETTOS

Mostly I prance around in stilettos
to keep alive and inspired,

as if there were still such
things as Paris hats and seamed

stockings, which in fact I am told
are making a comeback.

I pretend to live in black &
white, and flirt with the likes

of men named Victor and Peter
or Pet-ah, as Bette Davis would

blot her lipstick and say. This is
how it once was, half-lidded and smoky,

perfumed with attar of vermouth, stirred not
shaken. The usual regrets were somehow

smoothed over with plans for cocktails
tomorrow, my dearest darling,

and haven't we been
married, truly, truly married?

Ah, the mysteries evoked by such
phrases: the man and woman stuff—

the desperate kisses, the blowing leaves,
the calendar pages torn away;

My tears are dim sparkles caught
by a loving camera, accompanied

by shades of a sweet tenor sax,
a melancholy throb—

delicious, actually.

UNSEASONABLE

Coffee should not smell
better than it tastes;
this cup fills no emptiness.

There should be snow
that should pile softly,
hushing the clamors of everyday—
but it is a Monday morning
and the common ground is
seeded with confusion.

There should be a route
that should be open
enough to move on
when the night descends—
but the course has changed:
raging, unpredicted storms
have cratered all surfaces.

Listen to the radio:
a church burned down in Oakland,

another murder on the North Side;
more sleet predicted:
a report from the roadways—
how many are dead?

There should be spring
that should spring green
earnest life: seedlings, creatures,
babies—human and otherwise.
And then the crimes begin again
the slaughter of our sweet fictions,
the filch of what should be.

SISTER MARDI GRAS

If it keeps on rainin'
levee's goin' to break
and all these people have
no place to stay.
—Memphis Minnie, 1929

Old town never could decide
        whether it was soil or water,

hot city that celebrated death
        hosting jazz funerals,

dark place where cemeteries
        now lie under water,

swampy land that grew exquisite
        scandalous corruption,

violently strangled hostess
        of artists and crawfish and music:

Sister Woman hears your wounded voice, so sweet so hot so sweet
        and remembers how you shaped her.

She must sing and dance far, far away from you
        far from your watery grave,
    far from your fat drowned heart.

DINNER DATE

The man was justified, I admitted,
because he had served there.

I gave him that, anyway.

He'd been the soldier, and his soldiering
had to mean something. You could see

how much in those tight lips and his fist
squeezing the wine-glass stem, hard.

So I gave him that.

Then I told him Danny never came home.

I really laid it on:

24 years old, law school, Penn, his goodness,
sense of duty. The Navy pilot:

the way he was raised, how he was the first,
for me, the first and best,

and what it was like for us, the lush days
and the nights, summer after young summer.

I kept steaming on, juiced with the wine and some
strange rage: the obscenity never seemed

more obscene, this now old man still fighting
his black-hearted filthy military cause.

It was finally for nothing, I whispered, evilly.
Nothing. Your service, his death. Nothing.

He quit arguing. Shut up.
I felt queasy, like I stepped on something
and made it stop moving.

SISTER WOMAN

Rolling nowhere
Seeking nothing
At home in the rain
The gray morning cat
Curls up inside
Of herself.
Pet her or not
She won't flirt
With intruders
Like you.
She's a watcher:
She will see you
Offer everything
Green
And culled from
Your world
And her eyes will
Not blink
She's seen it before
And the heat
Is not safe
To her
Anonymous heart.

TULIPS

Tulips remind me
of Aunt Lil
who planted them
to relieve the terror
of that crumbling brick duplex
next door to the gas station
where she lived
her long narrow life.
Bulbous and pink and yellow
they were her babies,
her fruit that cannot
be eaten, but loved
as one can love flesh.
In the shivering winter
while they slept
she knitted their ripeness
into pillows as gifts.
These she sent into the world
hoping they would be
kindly received.

TELL ME, SISTER

Did you awaken before
cradle sleep ended?
Or did you grow breasts
over your heart
before you stopped
expecting .... everything?
Do you remember
the first heart-sting
that retold who you were?

Were you a ballerina before
You were a Black or a Jew?

How few wounds
does it take not to die?
Are your bleeding
places deeper?
Do you think
my lesions weep less than
yours or that
my skin protects me better?
Tell me, Sister,
Is your story more true
than mine?

VINEYARD

The Atlantic is blue gray
here, and clean.
The light, as Hopper saw it:
cool, elegant, a contradiction
in its intensity.
I think of myself as like
this light.

I was my best
here, in this windswept place.
I was with the sun
gleaming on your skin,
I knew the shape of your hands
as the sun did,
the curve of your body
against the waves of ocean.

Flesh fragrant, berry-like,
warmth dissolving coolness,
anguished edges, every shadow.

MAGICIANS

Who were you, who was I?
Were you bold,
descended of the *Maccabees*,
a lion-prince striding
among lesser men?

Was yours the flesh
of fruit so exotic
I trembled just to touch it?
Did your eyes
hold all the depth
of seas so azure blue
that I was lost?

Was I lost, lost,
a she-lamb
dissolving in that
blue enchanted light,
a creature caught
sailing to Atlantis?
Was I the fool
or the sorcerer
who created you,
invented you,
dressed you in magic,
loved you absurdly,
breathed you,
dreamed you.

GONE, GOOD-BYE, ENCORE

I am one who knows what
parting is,
the drawn and quartered
feel of it, the near-fatal tearing.

The word good-bye,
the word gone, are its
smallest prongs,
slivers of glass
working their sharp ways through
the flesh.

We loved each other once,
before the wounding.
Then Time,
that mad, voracious fiend
galloped by
devouring everything,
everything good
everything rotten.

Still
yesterday
by chance
we stood in a line
next to one another.
You nodded
your own nod,
half-sweet, half-public,
then off you went, and there they
were again, drawing blood again,
those jagged word-spikes,
those tiny stinging blades:

Gone. Good-bye.

PINK LADY

I reach back
because
you were there
part of the real
swing dancing
part of the innocent
erotic
sweet-knowing
never-doubting
worth-saving
world.
How is it I hear
the music
so clearly
when it was
so abundantly
yours?

Mama, my lipstick is red
my hair is upswept
my favorite shoes
have platforms
when I slide
into the role
of ghost, the delicious
game in which
your time becomes mine
and I can indulge
the parts of me
that long after
the dazzling
parts of you.

What could be better?
To smell like gardenias
wear low-cut black dresses
sip many cocktails,
smoke many Camels;
To never consider
that Martin or Phillip
might wish
more of us than
a kiss and a dance,
a Pink Lady romance;

Mama, we wet our lips
smooth our seams
bat our eyes
live our dreams
with so many men
we dance
the time away
knowing:
how wonderful
to be woman
what glamour tints
the nights,
what splendor gilds
the days....

Oh, Mother, I wonder
why must we
ever wake;
You, laughing woman,
the pinkest lady;
I, your chameleon child
dancing in the shadows.

DEAR JIM,

What force invaded the hollow chamber

that may have been

your heart? Was it a spade? Sharp?

Did it dig through pink pulsing matter,

separating layers and burning them to crisp gray char?

Was it poison, delivered by arrow from a pretty woman

who came to know you well? Did she sing a ballad?

Whistle? Stare out a window at the moon

as she stirred her dark liquid and poured

it boiling from a vat?

Were you already emptied of any flutter there,

or did she take it from you?

You walk the streets as I do, show up

at a few of the old places, look much the same.

Maybe you ought to ask

the wizard

to get you back a heart.

DEAR GUY,

A while ago you lodged
yourself inside the folds

of my flesh and seeped
into the fluid drip

of lymph or brine or bile
that courses to the brain.

You dragged along enough
flotsam of your self to become the

ever something I have in mind
as I turn the corners

of the town, but on Wednesday
when you slipped down from

your bottomless cerebral post and
leaped into my throat,

right there in front of Starbuck's
near your office

you surprised me as you sank
like a fireball into my chest

because I know full well
you still reside above and

not a hundred years of dreams
will make you ever leave, you bastard.

DEAR ALEX,

Every morning I awaken with all of the men:

they come back to me, milky gray as dawn,

nothing left of them now but what

the morning mind yields up:

old bones, a sackful, skeleton arms, knees

that dipped over dance floors crumbling

into a brain shaken by terrible dreams

of all of them lost, disintegrated to ash, B, L, S,

and you ask me to add you

to the index of bitterness, the panoply

of dust: your sweet-boy face, your fine-haired head,

clever lips, your firm little body that wants

and wants, even this. Do you dance bare-assed

under the moon? Strut like Napoleon? Consult

with wizards?

You're a half-mad fool

or just another hungry liar, I don't know which.

AIRBORNE

So he up and left you,
a stunning shock:

like expecting rest
in an innocent place,

a grassy mound,
touching pretty stones

that at once fly up,
smack your face hard,

enemy hard
completely unanticipated.

Of course he has gone crazy;
big bald head dripping

every screw loosened
into a shameful madness

that tells him the pilot is lying,
stalling, trying to whitewash

& and you who refuse to see
are complicit & part of the poison.

Travel brings it on,
the terrible screech & rush
of bodies and machines hurtling

place him on a spot
in the universe of experience
he can neither grip nor sustain;

he both caves in & lurches up
in the same moment,

a monster in spattered trousers
running from you, his great, great love.

BLACK SCAR

Scar, black scar,

the artist's long

black scar: symbol

in the earth

of the rip

in the body human

payment in flesh

all wars are economic

the cost charged   the poor;

black

the blood of Danny

long since

blackened, dried and caked;

oh Danny boy

who is no more,

he whom I loved we loved

the Ebert's older son

remember him?

he played a drum

the paper boy on Linden.

RAGE

in remembrance of the Sharpeville Massacre

It disturbs, this slanting light
yellow & rapturous
and once a part of promise.

Mocking now, and strange
these sighing palms
that stirred with expectation.

How like betrayal
the stillness of summer flowers
quiet, beautiful, unfaded.

I was not an alien here.
I was as one with the light
the palms, the lilies.

Why did the earth I loved
not cry out for me
as my life's blood
was sought and taken?

HEATHER

My sturdy little girl,
to whom were you loaned before me?

With which prince did you dance?
Through what streets did you ride?
Whose ancient eyes burned into yours
such knowing?

How is it you know to be
so at home in the sun
of this world,
so resolute, so beautiful, so free
a flower, a child so
poised to disappear,
as I never could,
into such a woman?

In what life did you learn?
What vanished star did you see?
My darling, who was your mother
before it was me?

OLD LOVES

The twin of myself
that I am in my mind
never parted from them,
those old loves;

we spend our days
walking through the home-town
places we knew,
the green streets where we played

under buckeye trees that
shed for us when we
were the tiny and masterful
collectors.

We scale the blueberry hills
covered with stones & carved markers
we learned not to fear,
race the elephant clouds

until mother calls and the sharp-edged
hour ends in a hush.

So this is an afterlife:
a pause without
& not without them,

a time to abide
not entirely lone
yet alone,

but not to dream; no,
our souls wait quietly,
closely crowded

on either side of this fluttering
opaqueness, this thin blue curtain,

& they know.
They know that I am coming.

JANUARY

Beyond the window
wind-driven snow,
down from Canada.
Trees like bones,
old black skeletons
shaking in pain.
I am alone and ill,
hiding here;
just a cold but I like
to say I never get them.
On my daughter's wall
Aunt Lil's petit point
little girl sits with her bunny
in a country field
while Aunt Lil herself
lies in a grave
I cannot find
somewhere out in Shaler;
my daughter's grown,
a woman now
making her life, tentatively,
but still
on her own.

Aunt Lil had a narrow life
but left these
vestiges in yarn: the little girl,
the tulips, the *talit* bag. Pieces of
herself for the children
who never look at them.
All is heat
the man of science said.
A mere moment's heat, at that.
The bunny in the field
is made of thread.
The little girl has gone away.
Try to stop smoking.
Take care of the cold.

RAVAGES

Life does not end.

This line was earned by sin,

this one by grief.

Both run deep

and permanent now,

like seams of coal

that can never be mined

but still scar the ground.

Mornings do come

birthing prospects

fragile and moist as shoots

breaking through dirt:

the possibility

of orchids, one more kiss,

another embrace,

even as the hours ebb

and chances drift off

into poems.

A CATHOLIC FUNERAL

for Patricia Dobler

Though young when she died,
Patricia had written with
an old woman's wisdom—
ideas multi-layered
for the hungry like flaky pastry
that yields more fullness with each bite.

A certain beauty, too,
deep, subtle, the kind it took eyes
fired by spirit to see;
the lucky saw what she allowed—
the intimate parts, body locations
that suffered, taut soul wrestling
with frenzy and raw death premonition.

My quarrel is not that she's gone,
but gone without a laurel crown,
or historical context; no words
for Patricia, except to remind us
she was a good Catholic girl.

No, all the praise that day
was for Messiah, when I longed
to hear her voice, to know her maiden name.

I APOLOGIZE

to my precious elders;
the valuable ones,
those thick-fleshed
indestructible Jews

I have known,
those who
endured; those who
had the clenched tooth
grit to flee before
the ovens were lit,
those—bergs and—steins
and—skis
those tailors artists bakers
peddlers scholars music-makers
who did not become the incinerated trash of Europe:

My own people, once stalwart as the stars,
must now weep as we, their stunning progeny,

disappear like shadows into the cracked cement of sweet
America
our brainless heads sucked under the white foam,
merging, whistling, forgetting, drowning, dancing,
no lessons learned, refusing to keep anything.

AUTOIMMUNITY

the body eats chunk by chunk
sips by mouth in bloody gulps
itself

the mind in disquiet scurries
finds sharp broken glass
free & perfect to pick at
itself

no flat of any hand
no fierce swipe defends
they rule & rip scream orders
are never disobeyed

embedded
shards in the brain
lips in the flesh writhe
& keep writhing

so we can say life is still alive
& this is the way we know it

NUMBNESS

is a visitor who asks
nothing,

but sits as though waiting.

She never wears color,
makes no particular

statement.

She arrived at the end
of a very long siege,

a war that ended
with no resolution.

I respect her veneer of
solidness, her calm eyelids,

her face made like stone.

I wish she would leave.

LEOPARDI AND ME

I have had a visitor,
an impervious spirit with a face
made like stone.
Her name is Numbness.
She sits and stares
with hard blind eyes. I have
wished she would leave.

Giacomo Leopardi calls her Noya.
He knows her precisely as I do,
but does not waste time making
wishes. He fights.

He knows where she came from.

She rode in on a backwash
pale dirty water in the wake
of the ship that carried off
the garden nymphs, the Jew Birds,
all the names I knew.

She preys upon me, chilling, hardening, prevailing.

He has his weapons, the ferocity of his heart.
Unlike me, he will not let her win.

HORNS

Much casual death had drained away their souls.
—Anthony Hecht

*No monument stands over Babi Yar. I am each old man
shot dead.*
—Yevgeny Yvetushenko

The deep primal knot
At the base of the skull
Does not think; one-eyed,
It sees only you.
You, with your horns.

Know this above all things:

It must take the horns from a beast
To bless its human self,
To ease its bones,
To secure its fragile borders.

Only then can it stop & chant a dirge,
A hymn of mourning for you;
Or make of you an ogre slayed
A rhyme, a song, a scalding tale of dread
To frighten tiny children.

YAD VASHEM*

Here bloom green
carob trees
sweet with spring;
the righteous few
are not forgotten
in Our Garden.
Silence pours
from leaf and vine.

Note the smooth
Stone shapes
amid the blossoms:
the sculpted mother's
arms around
her baby:
Tenderness,
the first remembrance
of the human artist.

Beyond the blossoms
his last remembrance,
Darkness:
the dying ashes, the
tiny flames that
burn eternal
within the concrete
and basalt.

*Yad Vashem is the name of the Holocaust Memorial in Jerusalem

A SURVIVOR'S CHILD PAINTS

for Valentin Lustig

The gray dead hover close
in this sweetly curving universe.

They dance and fly and sleep
among us and they wake,

bent travelers from
blue to yellow light.

Disturbed, they breathe the greening
smell of snails and rotting fishes,

yet smile them on their way
along a bloodless sea of flowers.

While Celan sways near us
someone feeds on soup, sups

a red rich broth of vibrant blood
not black milk;

and all these waters flow so clean
about us, unsalted by guilt or tears.

There is no blood upon these seas,
no sweat, no bile, no milk, no dew.

Priests, Hussars, Babies, Elders:
the dead and quick in the gardens

and on the waters, grip
hands to save each other.

We dream our morning noon nights
our trembling rabbits

our little boats cast off,
As we wait on lofty, fearful towers.

BITTER RAIN

This day could surely
use some wetting down.
The rain gods are trying; they should.

Dank as Hell on Devonshire,
red oaks made over, a black labyrinth
netting the old mansions.
They're trying hard to make rain; they should.

This day a Polish lady,
tiny, sharp-eyed, shrill,
speaking about her long-
past youth—throwing
rock-filled snowballs

at wounded German
prisoners on parade
at last in rubbled Cracow.

As the iron clouds burst
Reporting how the Krauts bled,
What she screamed:

This is for my father!
This is for my sister!
This is for my Warsaw!

Rain comes, pours. Nothing washes away.

THIS STORY

My child will visit Europe, ride trains,
rest under graceful trees,
swing along old boulevards,
wide and sun-dappled;
there may be music in the streets, fiddles
and concertinas. I see her beside wrought iron fences,
the light
is filtered sunlight, lemony, barely warm;
she is watching the prancing young Europeans
in their health, in their youth, in their blond beauty,
in their cities; they prance for peace, no nukes, no war,
        no more,
and no more. I think: All their cities, all the trains,

all the trees, all the wide boulevards, all the rotting
        underneath,
all the rotting cities, rotting spires, rotting fences
        rotting.

Year after year I could not address those losses.
I was a far-off daughter, safe, saved, new-born, lucky.
So lucky in sweet America that I had no right. No right to
        speak.
I wondered: What is the worst part? The animal part?
The shame of the animal part:
the round-up, the nakedness, the nothingness, the exposure,
the branding, the prodding of innocent flesh, the exposure
        of shame,
the red shame of bloody flesh?

I have no right, but I ask:
was the shame, the moaning, naked red shame, worse than
        the pain?

And where are all the Jews now, where have they gone?

They do not stroll the leafy boulevards; they do not grow up,
they do not grow old, grow anything; they do not wait, they
    do not sing;

they do not fight for their country's armies any more.

Is there a special place reserved for them?

They left these grand cities of arches & soaring steeples
    by way of chimneys.

Parents, uncles, cousins, arms, legs, sisters, tailors,
    scholars, thieves,

gamblers, the brown-eyed, the blue, riders, racers,
    red-heads, teachers, orphans,

tap-dancers, their feet, the drinkers, abstainers,
    brothers, actors, the wise,

the most and least beloved, the fools, *les autres,*
    the prayerful many and the few:

changed from pink flesh to ash, dirty grey ash, they flew
    away, they left us

to wonder about them in the early day and with the night's
    last thoughts

to twist & wonder, in our beds, to weep & grow fierce,

awake with resolution: to remember: no songs, no relief,
    this story.

EARLY ON I CAME

to love the rain,
the blue-grayness of it,
the drear and shine.
Liked to say I was raised
on rain, grew up on it
like every other plucky weed
every blade of scrubgrass.

The rain was mine
as was the day,

each day, and then
the sudden moon
appeared to follow me,
to ride steady, close
and silver on my shadow.

Now I know to never
seek more of them than this.
For my sake
I must stand mute, too,
above the grave

of the little ruby-throated bird.
I will not cry in autumn.
I will try to match the silence.

MIND AND THE BONES

Never mind the connection
wholeness is oneness

as in elephant there is trunk
in monkey his tail
we have within this bag of blood

a heart
a set of guts
this brain

in restless love

with borders categories
brain yearns to define:

black and white
&
sometimes color

brain must create
charts graphs thinking machines

in its image

in its irony

of crisscrossed lines
it conceives

misconnection disconnection reconnection

to its flesh

its joyful bones

its home

itself

its own fine self.

TO WRITE

I want to write
something for your
old Daddy who
doesn't hear birds
unless they shriek;
whose food passes
an untasting tongue
and whose heart seems
scabbed-over but
is exactly the same;
I want to touch him,
remind him
of scented things,
of beginnings—
I want to hear him say:
Yes, my darling,
I remember:
they were purple
and luscious,
my expectations,
the lilacs,
my lucky days.

POOR BENNIE

Although he senses a random universe
he keeps trying to describe the stars.

Silver filigree from mother's lamp
invades his brain through the prism of a teardrop.

He envies the fabled loner, the dreamer, the pretenders
in black raincoats, the famous tragedian, the clown.

He will twist along grotesque furrows,
A fool expecting answers, an ending to confusion

Until within cold shadows he'll hide away,
curled and begging comfort of the blinding, careless moon.

TRANSLUCENCE

We scribblers make careful note

of any hue we come upon:

Hope's green nose pokes

through weary garden dirt;

Joy's fat laughter rolls,

jiggling and pink;

Proud Mary's blue blood stalls—

the body can't keep a secret.

Look, the little handwriting lady

already has a jump on those

gunmetal bands that hold your neck

in place and guide your fingers.

They're an extension, down your arm,

through your hand, of the heaviness piled above.

LESSON

Your teaching
tool   is your tongue
formerly tender
warm   when it wanted
what it wanted;
now a jagged pick
you drive   straight
into my chest;
my throat too is caught
and something soft
just below   the bone
seems to tear
with each cruel word
and at once
I understand
why they call this
absurd   condition   heartbreak.

BED AND BREAKFAST

My head is clamorous this morning.
Before me clowns are trampling the pathways.

Hard-wired with lust & hunger,
they rush
to kitchen tables.

If fed, well and quickly,
they will use an ordinary spoon.

If denied, they will choose the knife.

THE HUMAN WAVE

1

Before, unwarned, the children
tread the plain, welcomed morning,
the sweet green pathways revealed
to them by mother Hope.

They fed at her breast each new day,
spreading their lips, pounding their bodies
in deep reverence; this was not unhealthy,
it was sound, & what the mother wished.

In gratitude
the children prostrated themselves.
In love, they clung to her, offering their voices
ringing with song and verse, their quickened, beating
hearts in anthems.

2

In health they did not suspect her
vast, dark secret could be birth solely for its own sake.
Beloved she, who seemed to give so much, fled from them
as the poisonous wave rose and raged and tore asunder.

Caught, the daughters quickly cried out, weeping
for the mother, pitifully weeping;
her sons cried too, beat their chests, and begged
for strength and answers.

The mother paused and shrugged.
This blinking took an instant.
Then cruelty bled to indifference
in her bright cold eye
as it closed completely upon the lost.

3

Yet—shorn, fragmented, and regurgitated,
in time the living remnant dares
to flutter anew, and call out
to her, slowly, because they must;
to once more seek Hope, their mother,
despite her silence, her hideous silence,
despite the star-swept void.

SONGS

1

for Katherine Finestone

Joy came marching an apple and American flag
in grand celebration;
our tunes out-sang the radio all night.
I remember softness, arms and breasts
around me in a bed, then nothing;
a snapshot of a woman who looks
like me now
staring into the veiled distance
with tilted eyes, thin shapely lips, a square jaw.

2

for Dora Ruttenberg

So much more music than speech—
songs from a girlhood, *a Grand Old Czar,*
Meet Me in Saint Louie, Louie, meet me at the fair.
We sat and rocked in a swing on a porch.
She held my pretty little hand in her warm,
worn-down fingers.
Wishes for a future whispered in Yiddish,
A melody sung as part of a prayer.
Afternoons hummed with raisins and almonds
& pictures of relatives who were disappearing;
& there was tea in the cupboard, lemon pie in the fridge.

3

Since, over seasons of
grace and of mourning
riding the raging horse of time
I hung onto these
tiny gleaming nugget-notes
imbedding them in bone so deep,
they are mine, they are me.

KNOWINGS

There are knowings
You deny me:
the wisdom of
a gentle cow,
the purple cowslip,
a graceful dove.
The certainty
of a storm,
the busy sycamore,
its sap,
its falling bark.

What I do
is plant tomatoes,
will them
to redden, believing
they are mine.
Here, in this field
where willows
wave against
a silent sky,
I am all my
yearnings,
foolish
in ways which
they are not.

FOR GATES & JOBS & SEISMIC SHIFTS

Buddy Holly's dead these many years,
so are Kennedy, Kerouac and Kesey.
Now there's nearly no one
left bored enough to speak up
for the gimlet, or flying down to Rio..

But what about the small sad sacks lost
in the rock n' rollin' world those shadow kids
who never got the message right?
Losers marked by the
Scotch tape on their glasses
and their terrible fat asses
jokes to the others
the cool-man-cools in hot dark shades and flip-flops…

Did the shut-outs console themselves spilling
tales of woe in coffee joints?
Did they find love in any of their glum places?

Whoa! A nanosecond! Please!
Resurrection plastic, circuits open.
A tale of shifting fortunes: Of randomness
and fickleness, of clicks instead of bricks
and making it with pockets full of change.

Off with Elvis are the glamour girls
in their in gold high-heels
lipstick blots on filter-tips.
Gone too the soft guitars that strummed
on palm-treed, pink-sand beaches.

DANCING IN THE GARDEN

Without words but not voice
the coyote faces the evening stars
and calls out to heaven.

An easy wind carries his howl.

Without tools but not hunger
the koala feeds on the ripe trees,
the seeds & fruits & green of the earth.

The earth opens her warm mouth to him.

Without weapons but not strength
the elephant will fight but never seek
in sport to maim its own.

The herds huddle in the night.
They commit no atrocities on one another.

Without instruments but not music
the antelope hears the deep rhythms
of love and mates.

The female accepts the male or she does not.
There may be sounds, keening. There is no rape.

Without confusion but not without spirit
they roam, free and at home
in the glittering garden.

MAIDEN AUNT ESCAPES

She of gentle home-bound feet
—not by clay but cloth—
recasts black and white, technicolor threads
into the exotic wildland of dreams:
star-strung galaxies
to fly through whole and to return,
skimming waterways and fabled granite cities.

Bits of Lillian's sadness:
only her own hands
to soothe peach-scented cream
on thinning skin;
the left hand that trembles,
the skin brown and dotted as an owlet's wing;

a photograph kept under starched sheets,
Clark Gable, his dazzling, crooked smile,
hidden from the sight of sister Ruth;

and next to Clark rests Lillian in sepia,
at eighteen, looking dreamy,
up and away from the camera,
ready to begin the life that never comes.

Only fantasy is treasure,
the careful gift she never shares,
but unlocks in the great darkness
so as not to grieve too long,
to welcome the deeper sleep that comes.

LOKI

In the stirring leaves
We can hear the tree speak;
It asks to live, to not be slain
By the axe, to die old
In a sweet whisper,
As promised.

But there are axes
Hidden in plain sight, murderers
Who wield them and smile.
They reap with pleasure.
Praise the hardwood,
Take the day.

Caught in love's silky
Chords, the he and she writhe
Toward perfect union;
Humans stumbling with desire
Yearning for the dance.
The dance that never ends,
As promised.

We loved each other once,
Unaware there was immolation in it.
Immolation in the dance,
Fire too much to bear.
We consumed and were consumed
Day and night after night
Consummation in blue fire
As the little Loki leapt
And the little Loki laughed.

ROSES

The simple rose,
born into radiance,
never hides
nor eludes her admirers;
not lulled
by thorn's protection
she doesn't even try;
dazzling, disarming,
she bursts forth
in briefest beauty
petals blushing
fuchsia pink, carmine blood.

Rita Rose flashes
across dreamscapes,
supple in glitter
real enough
for old men lost,
long-gone from Hope,
for young men hot,
far-gone from Good Intent.
She undulates in reddest silk,
parts carmine lips,
flutters violet lids,
bends deeply into the camera,
rewards every bit of love she can.

ANOTHER THING

opening a new white page
the machine says CREATE
& something in a back corner
of the brain schlepps
its weary self up
and announces this feels
a little like buying
a lottery ticket
yes for a few moments
there is this bright-faced
thing giggles & jiggles
but then of course
it winks & settles back
under the old couch
with the stained upholstery
which is where it
often goes to sleep. (~.~)

REENTRY

ponies bow down
yellow teeth bared
nostrils spread wide

I
  an acrobat
     tumble
       crash

struggle to right myself

ponies bow down
yellow teeth bared
nostrils spread wide

blackbirds overtake

     the grey-veined night

carousel horses spin on
blue yields purple to green to gold
edges blend and blur

ponies bow down
yellow teeth bared
nostrils spread wide

rear back

full circle

liquid dissolves

reconstitutes hard

wounds will heal over

but flesh swells

the scar is pink but not pretty—
—a most unlikely rose
—a calcified rose

HEAVEN

I hope to kiss both my grandmothers,
who I have missed all my life,
to have them cradle & comfort me,
as curled in their arms
and no longer numb, I cry.

I cry as I am rocked back & forth
and passed between them;
my grandmothers' hands stroke my skin
until the ravages of life
that have marked me,
float away & I am pink & tender
& new as first wildflowers.

Then my grandmothers croon
the truth, a cadence sweet & simple,
and at once the onionskin layers
of mind-papering are peeled away
and the confusion that reigned
shoots high & away & scatters,
buck-shot confetti swirling in bright blue air.

And then, unscarred & clean, I understand.
I know why one soul was born—*lean & blessed,
supple & strong: Joe DiMaggio*—!
& sent to this earth on the exact same day
as Jimmy Jones, who came
to our door each June, blind and nodding
in unmatched plaids,
arrived to tune the old player piano.

Everything is explained: my grandmothers
tenderly place each note of precious truth
in a hollowed green melon, carved into a basket
I can carry, and we are blown home, completely;
and all is just as it should be
and never, until this moment, was.

HOME

I always kept the children's work
on the refrigerator door—
their drawings of spindly people,
little red houses with tulips
rising higher than the rooftops,
suns with smiling faces,
spelling tests and math papers
sporting gold stars and animal stickers.
That was the center
of what we had, that kitchen,
its faux-marble countertops,
the bright windows and the window screens,
the inevitable world to come just beyond--
but there, near us, the sweetgum trees,
beautiful in every season,
leaves blazing purple and orange in autumn,
heavy branches iced and white in winter.
Did I mention how smart the kids were?
Or how the memory swallows like Chianti,
the whisper of sweetness, the bite in the throat.

URBANITY

how to tolerate crowds
of human strangers
all those bodies that sweat
and push and displace
space and air and seats
on buses or clog the roadways
I don't mean robbers
rapists or molesters
or anything like that
I mean the strangers who
load up on wine in restaurants
and scream their shrill
heads off when you are trying to eat
the ones who smell lousy
that you have to wait behind
in long lines at the store
the ones who run red lights
and cut you off in traffic
and what about all the pretending
that goes on? One honest curmudgeon
said hell is other people but few
will admit that is the truth
nor will most admit a reasonable
preference for dogs.

SONG FOR THE END
OF LITHUANIAN JEWRY

Not a charm of goldfinches swirling away
not a clamor of crows in warning
not the sad voice of Kovner,
labeled the fool, urging escape
could penetrate the rays of sunset
striking the leaded glass windows
or find place upon the snowy linens,
or among the crystal wine cups
or golden candles glowing
on the Sabbath table.
No dire word dare enter the quiet after prayers,
the men somber, hushed, still rocking
with praise for the Almighty, and then
the women's dance, their swaying steps,
their rosy children, their clean, kosher homes.
The only bittersweet this night are notes of the violin.

AGAINST LOSS

there is depletion allowance
a hollow gray chamber
where certainty once dwelt.
My best pal had presence—
he had young adventures
and disappointments—
more even than
the every hair counted
on his fearless crown.
Once we kibitzed around
our magic places—
laughed so much of the time
because through wise blue eyes
he could see the silliness wrapped
in slyness and could drown me
in the universe of the slaphappy
whenever he wanted.
June is the cruelest month for me.
Warm, sunlit, grievous
June.

AGAINST LOSS #2

We don't know the proof,
we don't even care
it's buttery we want, not oaky, please.
We want the slow buzz up
the route we take that turns
the oddest palest face to beauty
that dims the awful march of days,
of foolish longings and lousy love
long gone wrong anyway.
All that was meant to be
better than this
can be reassigned
for about twenty dollars,
a blessed bargain
if you think of baby powder,
crystal meth or anything injectable.

MODNE TEG, MODNE NACHT

The young abandon day for dreamy night
eager beneath the yellow moon
rolling with simple pleasure.

Wrapped in moments of flesh
they seem to soar above the lion and the lamb.
They glimpse beyond the blowing stars.

They believe in the gorgeous present.

Do they know that other days will follow?
Strange days. Strange nights.
Moons will grow dim and blacken.
Seas will yearn and rise.

Suns will bear down, over-heating land,
bleaching away what grows,
disrupting the ordered song.

Unease will creep in, then blanket.

After fits of nervy eruption,
hemming and speculation,
there will be no more cries to you,
no further trust that you will hear.

The one left waiting to disappear
by morning will find confusion
in the tight green buds,
oddness in the celebration.

TEACH ME TO TANGO

Because they feel
& weep & say so
I hear confessionals
that tell me all about
being black   being Jew
being Asian   being Greek
being woman   being waitress
being alone   being small
being man   being scared
being old   being ill
being poor,   for example.

Because they crave catharsis
I am privy to
the worst   the best
remembering   forgetting
crawling   flying
lust   numbness
parents   partners
failure   falsehood
confusion   chaos
wholeness   fragmentation.

Where is the red-tailed hawk,
the yellow moons of yesternights...

the meadow, the mountain, the marigolds;

I need the mysteries of sea-glass, spirits,
& the eucalyptus tree...

Bring me bunches of lavender and lillies,
lemons in a crystal bowl.

I seek the music, I search for the muse.
Sing to me of ecstacy. Teach me to tango.